YOUR KNOWLEDGE HAS VALUE

Anderson Brians

An analysis on "Business Strategy and Management Control measures for success"

GRIN Verlag

Bibliografische Information der Deutschen Nationalbibliothek:

Die Deutsche Bibliothek verzeichnet diese Publikation in der Deutschen National-
bibliografie; detaillierte bibliografische Daten sind im Internet über http://dnb.d-
nb.de/ abrufbar.

Imprint:

Copyright © 2012 GRIN Verlag GmbH
Druck und Bindung: Books on Demand GmbH, Norderstedt Germany
ISBN: 978-3-656-39860-8

This book at GRIN:

http://www.grin.com/en/e-book/211923/an-analysis-on-business-strategy-and-
management-control-measures-for-success

GRIN - Your knowledge has value

Der GRIN Verlag publiziert seit 1998 wissenschaftliche Arbeiten von Studenten, Hochschullehrern und anderen Akademikern als eBook und gedrucktes Buch. Die Verlagswebsite www.grin.com ist die ideale Plattform zur Veröffentlichung von Hausarbeiten, Abschlussarbeiten, wissenschaftlichen Aufsätzen, Dissertationen und Fachbüchern.

Visit us on the internet:

http://www.grin.com/

http://www.facebook.com/grincom

http://www.twitter.com/grin_com

'Business Strategy and Management Control measures for success'

DECLARATION

This research dissertation is my original work and has not been presented to any other examination body. No part of this research dissertation should be reproduced without my consent or that of the institution.

Name..

Sign: _____ Date: _____

Declaration by supervision

This research dissertation has been submitted by my approval as institution supervisor.

Lecturer Supervising

Name:

Sign: _____ Date:_____

DEDICATION

I dedicate this project to my dear parents Mr. and Mrs. ....who, with their dedicated effort made me attain this level of hard achievement? My caring colleagues in this lovely institution whose concern cannot go unmentioned for their understanding lobe, support and strength throughout this noble course, they have been amazing enabling me to be where I am today.

I truly love you all.

ACKNOWLEDGEMENT

My sincere thanks go to the Almighty God for giving me healthy and peace of mind throughout my studies. I am specially thanking my supervisor …………..for good advice, guidance, patience and dedication during this research dissertation. He offered me technical advice that I directly needed during this work.

To my parents for financial support and encouragement , my entire family for challenging me academically also to my former classmates …………..just to mention but a few for always telling me not to give up when the going was tough during this course.

Approval Page

This applied dissertation was submitted by _____ under the direction of the persons listed below. It was submitted to the _____ School of _____ and approved in partial fulfillment of the requirements for the master's degree of _____ at _____ University.

_____   _____

Date   Committee Chair

_____   _____

Date   Committee Member

_____   _____

Date   Program Professor Review (*Applied Research*

Center)

_____   _____

Date   Associate Dean for Research and Evaluation.

Abstract

This research will be an analysis ' on Business Strategy and Management Control measures for successes of business organizations. It will also look at the strategic management tools that are needed for an organization to achieve competitive advantage.

The research has been divided into parts and the first part is the introductory part which outlines and elaborates on the topic of study. The second part is the background which is the main section of the research. The background part explains further on the topic of study and also elaborates the different management tools that are applied by business organizations to achieve competitive advantage.

The literature review which gives the theoretical view from other researchers and authors on the very topic of the study and it also looks at other areas that have been covered by other previous researches.

The part on the research outlines the various methods used in data collection and how data was will be collected from the respondents.

Strategic management tools

Introduction

This excerpt will look at the issue of business strategy and management control measures for the success of business organizations and corporate entities. It will identify the various management tools and control methods that organizations put in place to achieve a competitive advantage over their competitors. It will also identify the strategic business solutions that businesses employee in the competitive and dynamic business environment (Polyack, &Jolene. 2004, p 78).

Background of the study

To deduce a better understanding of this topic it is essential that the terms strategy and management tools are well understood. The word strategy can be defined as the game plan of how one intends to achieve something, that is, it is the tactic of doing something with the aim of achieving some goals. Management tools are the operational devices or ways of managing organizations activities (Canales, J & Barbara, 2000, p 90).

Strategic management tools are the devices of management that help the organization to come up with proper methods for business operations to attain strategic advantage over their competitors. The role played by the management tools is to enhance the capability of the business in analyzing the prevailing market conditions. This offers a suitable opportunity to the clientele to assess the wide assortment of products as well as services that are offered by the firm. These are the tools that form the fundamental part of the game plan in coming up with a smart operation strategy (Hamel, & Gary, 2009, p 45).

Businesses have to develop strategic management tools to be able acquire a competitive edge, be able to cope in the dynamic business environment and more importantly to be to bench mark with other well doing businesses in the industry.

Strategic business solutions are only successful they results in a product or service, which sells well. Strategic Management Tools help analyze the market in which you are positioned. They are the devices that help the business to evaluate market conditions and changes in the external environment. It is a clear business strategy that will enable a firm to achieve the economic responsibilities that the society expect from it these include satisfy the consumers with products, create new wealth, create new jobs, promote innovation and generate revenues from their operations. This creates the opportunity to offer clients a range of products that are more competitive than those of the competitors and better adapted to market developments. The major strategic management tools include (Allison, & Kaye.2005, p 123).

Porter's Five Force.

The implication of the model of Five Forces of Porter is a procedure that is applicable in the analysis of a business environment in an organization along with the industrial context whose foundation is key aspects that shape the sector namely; competitors, the new entrants, the substitute products, the consumers as well as suppliers (Carrigan, &Linda, 2005, p 205).

New Entrants;

Every industry portends the possibility of attracting new firms depending on its profit prospects. This slowly changes the market type through a continuum of monopolistic to perfect competition. The various barriers to entry are the following:

➢ Economies of scale: economies of scale are the cost advantages that enterprises obtain due to size, with cost per unit of output generally decreasing with increasing scale as fixed costs are spread out over more units of output. Often operational efficiency is also greater with increasing scale, leading to lower variable cost as well. Economies of scale are achieved when there is an increase in the volume of production for a decrease in the marginal cost of production (Collett, & Stacey, 2006, p 123).

➢

➢ Brand loyalty~ Brand loyalty is where a person buys products from the same manufacturer repeatedly rather than from other suppliers. It consists of a consumer's commitment to repurchase or otherwise continue using the brand. It can be demonstrated by repeated buying of a product or service, or other positive behaviors such as word of mouth advocacy. In brand loyalty there is a built trust in the products or services, and the consumers are not ready to change their mind or behavior towards the product or service.

➢ Government Regulation ~ a regulation is *a* rule or order having the force of law, prescribed by a superior, relating to the actions of those under the authority's control. Regulation can take many forms: legal restrictions promulgated by a government authority, contractual obligations that bind many parties, self-regulation by an industry such as through a trade association, social regulation ,co-regulation, third-party regulation, certification, accreditation or market regulation.

➢ Customer Switching Costs ~ the negative costs that a consumer incurs as a result of changing suppliers, brands or products. Although most prevalent switching costs are monetary in nature, there are also psychological, effort- and time-based switching costs.

- ➤ Cost Advantage – this is can be defined as the ability to produce goods or services at the reduced cost of production lower than of the rival firms in the same industry. Cost advantage is achieved with efficiency in production at the lowest cost possible.
- ➤ Ease in distribution ~ the strategic location of a company in relation to the market position dictates its distribution costs. Good and efficient distribution channels make it easy for the products to reach the target customer and at a lower cost (Collett, & Stacey, 2006, p 289).

The competitors;

Hostility among competing firms in an industry in their endeavors to increase market share puts profitability at risk. The ability of a company to survive under these conditions depends on the bargaining power of buyers and sellers.

Bargaining Power of Buyers;

Buyers are the consumers of a firm's products. They may be the final consumers or the distributers. Bargaining power of buyers is the ability of a consumer to negotiate for price cuts or increase in the quality of products and services. This in turn reduces a company's profitability. It may also result into the increment of operation costs. In this way, they are regarded as a threat (Goold, & Michael, 2008, p 234).

Bargaining Power of Suppliers;

Suppliers are the firms or individuals who provide an industry with the raw materials for production. Bargaining power of the suppliers is the ability of these suppliers to raise the market prices of production inputs. The risk is multiplied when the suppliers monopolize the market.

Substitute products;

Substitute products are products and services in the market with similar satisfying ability to the consumers. A company's ability to raise a product's price depends on the number of close substitutes in the market. This ultimately bears a direct effect on a company's profitability.

The influence of Porter's five forces varies from business to business. However, regardless of the industry, these five forces influence the prices, the costs, and the capital investment necessary for break through and growth in any industry. Managers therefore need to understand this model before implementing strategic decisions. It is also vital in the comprehension of market structures. This ultimately aids in the formulation of suitable business policies and achievable development agenda (Gottfredson, 2006, p 108).

The BCG Growth Share Matrix a forecasting tool that is portfolio oriented. The BCG depends on the observation that a company's business can be categorized into four divisions depending on the blend of market growth and market shares comparative to the major competitor. In this case, market growth acts as a substitute for industry attractiveness, while the comparative market share acts as a substitute for competitive advantage. The whole assumption behind this type of a matrix model is that a comparative increase in market share will result in a comparative increase in cash flow. Logically speaking, the matrix can be relied upon because, when a firm increases its market share it implies that it is consolidating its advantages to overcome its competitors and has the great opportunity to have a cost advantage over them. The other factor to defend this reasoning behind the matrix is that as the market expands, investments in assets also increases and thus overall increase in cash utilization. Conclusively, the position of the business on the matrix is an indication of cash creation and its cash utilization. For instance those Strategic Business Units (SBUs) that are expanding rapidly can be financed by those business units that are at their maturity stage and are capable of producing a lot of cash. If a business can develop rapidly by venturing to become the market leader in a swiftly expanding market, the business is able to relocate along the matrix and adopt a cost advantage strategy (Gottfredson, 2006, p 28)

The BCG model has therefore come up with four categories of business units between which different portfolios can be compared. These categories include

Dogs: These symbolize those business units with low market share and a low growth rate. Dogs cannot generate cash and in equal measure they cannot utilize large amount of cash. Dogs however hold a lot of cash that is held up in the business with little utilization. Dogs are the categories of businesses that should be considered for divestiture.

Questions marks: These are businesses that are developing swiftly and utilize large a mount of cash. However, question marks have low market share and thus they are not capable of producing a lot of cash. A question mark has all the space and opportunity for growth, metamorphose into a star. It can also deteriorate easily into a dog in cases of slow market growth rate. Question marks need a thorough scrutiny to ascertain whether the investment made into them is of necessity (Polyack, &Jolene. 2004, p 112).

Stars: These are the businesses that have become market leaders. They produce a lot of cash because of their strong comparative market share. Stars also utilize large amount of cash because of the high growth rate. When stars keep acquiring large market shares, they generate into cash cows, with decrease in growth rates. For a good business portfolio, stars are necessary for they will become cash cows and be to produce cash for the business (Goold, & Michael, 2008, p 90).

Cash cows are businesses that have become market leaders in a mature market. They show a return on assets of the business that is higher above the market growth rate, hence produce more cash than they can utilize. Cash cows act as major sources of funds for investing into question marks to become the stars. They also provide cash for operations, administrative expenses and for research and development. They also help the business to pay its debts. Businesses use the discounted cash flow analysis to determine the value of cash cows at any given time.

The SWOT matrix which is an analysis of (Strengths, Weaknesses, Opportunities, and Threats) enables the organization to evaluate it environment both internal and external with an aim of achieving a good operation strategy for competitive advantage. It is very important because it enables an organization to identify specific areas that need improvement or areas that need more capacity enhancement to increase productivity and profitability for the business (*Pl*Collis,& Daniel , 2008, p 112)

Strengths emerge from those particular activities or assets that enable the business to achieve a competitive edge over its competitors. The sources of strengths for a business can be

- ➢ Good distribution channels
- ➢ Good promotional mix

- ➤ Quality products
- ➤ Customer/brand loyalty
- ➤ Economies of scale
- ➤ Good organizational management

Weaknesses are the loopholes that can easily lead to the collapse of a business. Weaknesses are emerge from the internal affairs of the organization

- ➤ Sources of weaknesses include
- ➤ Obsolete or outdated technology
- ➤ High rate staff of turn over
- ➤ Weak distribution channels for the products
- ➤ Absence of Research and Design
- ➤ Poor organizational management
- ➤ Poor customer service
- ➤ Debt burdens

Opportunities are circumstances that are available in the external environment and a business can easily make good use of them for a competitive advantage. Opportunities in the external environment can be a reduction in the tax rate which an organization can take advantage of to reduce the production cost.

Threats also emerge from the external environment. Threats for a business can be from sources such as political instability within a nation, high tax regime that can increase the cost of doing business. Economic conditions such as inflation which can raise the cost of production. The most common sources of threats are

- Unmanned expansion
- Emergence of new products
- Presence of substitute products
- New Markets
- New products in the market
- Political instability
- Unstable revenues

The marketing strategy revolves around the popular marketing mix known as The 4 P's of the Marketing Mix. This mix, looks at the individual elements that are involved in the sales and marketing activities of a product. The 'P's are Product, Price, Place and Promotion. These are the elements that are used in market segmentation, market targeting and product positioning.

Taking at a closer look at each of the individual 'P's, product refers to the actual offering that the marketer is providing to the consumers in the market. The product must have the ability to satisfy and meet the consumers' needs. It should be of the right quality with the required conditions that the consumer desire from it.

Price being a function of the production and all the activities involved in getting the product into the market is another important element in the marketing mix. Price is arrived after putting into consideration the cost of production, advertisement or promotion and distribution of the product. It is one of the very important elements of the marketing mix (Goold, & Michael, 2008, p 90).

Place (distribution, sales)

This is of the important marketing mix that ensures that the product is readily available in the market for the consumers. Distribution should well channel to ensure that the product is able to reach a many consumers at the right time and at the lowest cost possible. The channels of distribution should be properly organized to promote high sales volume to generate high sales revenue hence high profitability (Goold, & Michael, 2008, p 63).

Promotion (communication, marketing)

To create product awareness and thus increase the sales volume for a particular product, promotion is therefore deemed paramount. Promotion enables the customers to obtain information about the products that the marketer is offering; they are also able to learn more about the products features and functionalities. Promotion is mainly done to increase product awareness and increase sales. The various types of promotion are advertising and personal selling.

Recent studies have asserted the 4 'P's of marketing mix can be increased to 7 'P's whereby other P's include People to whom the products are to be sold to, Physical which is determined by the experience from the consumer about the product and finally Process, especially how a service is offered.

The Product Lifecycle Analysis is an assessment tool that is applied by a business organizations to evaluate the sales performance of a product or service in the market place, this assessment is a tactical strategy to enable the organization see the performance of the product or service in the market and make appropriate marketing decisions that will ensure increased sales volume and increase product acceptance among its consumers (Goold, & Michael, 2008, p 63).

The analysis of product life cycle is very important to enable the business know the stages and their impacts on the overall sales. These stages are

➢ Introduction

➢ Growth

➢ Maturity

➢ Decline

Introduction

At this stage, the product is very new and not many consumers are aware of its existence in the market. At this stage, the sales are low, profits are also very low this due to the fact that not many consumers know the product. At the introduction stage, the marketing strategies to be applied are advertising, and modifying the products to improve its features and qualities.

Growth

This the stage that is market by increasing sales as more and more consumers becomes aware of the product. There are also few competitors offering the same product. Profits also increase at this stage and sales revenue is also increasing. The business has invested in promotion and the more channels of distribution have been opened to ensure the product reaches the market. the marketing strategy to be used at this stage is advertising to ensure the product awareness among the consumers is increased. There is also need to identify new distribution channels to increase product market penetration.

Maturity

This is the stage where sales have reached the optimum level, profits start declining with subsequent decline in sales volume. There is also increasing competition from the other producers of similar products. At this stage, all the channels of distribution have been fully utilized and thus slow movement of the product.

Decline

As the name suggest, this is the stage that is characterized by decline in sales volume, sales revenue and profitability. This stage is also characterized by intense competition from other similar products. At the decline stage the market has become over saturated with products from the competitors, the strategies at this stage to enable the product come out the decline stage is the identification of the new markets. In new markets, there are consumers who are searching for the products to meet their needs (Hamel, & Gary, 2009, p 45).

Ansoff Matrix is a model for marketing which relies on new or existing products or markets. In each of these marketing strategies there are various stages of risk. It is the matrix that enables the organization to come up the best marketing strategy; it explores the possibilities of having new products in new markets, or existing products in existing markets. The strategy if applied appropriately enables the organization to market its products or services more efficiently and emerge the market leader.

These strategies include the following

1. Market penetration: This is strategy is aimed at expanding the market share inside the existing market sections, attained by selling more of the products to identified customers or alternatively discovering new customers inside the existing markets.

2. Product development: This strategy aims discovering new products for already in place markets. The strategy helps to identify the ways of marketing the new product and ways of overcoming competitors.

3. Market development: The strategy is aimed at discovering new markets for already in place products. In this case the products are already in existence. To identify new markets, proper market research and development is therefore deemed paramount.

4. Diversification: The strategy involves the transition of new products into new markets concurrently. This strategy comes with a great level of risk since its implementation comes with more uncertainties.

Abraham Maslow is considered as one of the greatest motivation theorist for having come up with the hierarchy of needs. According to him he arranged these needs in order of hierarchy, forming a pyramid known as the pyramid of needs.

Maslow's pyramid has been used by business organizations to rank the human needs and help in the process of motivation. According to Maslow human needs can be ranked in order of high hierarchy starting from the lower level needs to higher level needs. According to him human needs are divided into two main groups, mainly the lower level needs and the higher level needs. Lower level needs are those that are basic and therefore must be satisfied first before one can proceed to the higher level needs. The category of the lower level needs include the following love, safety and security, and self esteem. The category of higher level needs also called development or growth needs include; recognition self-actualization and aesthetics. The high level needs drive individuals towards the attainment of self actualization; that is everybody struggles for recognition and the opportunity to prove his or her worth in handling issues. These needs can therefore be ranked as follows (Drucker, & Peter F 2009, p 309).

1) Biological and physiological needs, these include food, air, shelter, drink, food and sleep
2) Safety and security needs, these range from provision of safety environment free from any invasion of whatever kind.
3) Love needs, these needs are based on the assumption that man is a social animal by nature and therefore needs to love and beloved back by others.

4) Esteem needs these needs relate to the achievements, prestige social status and assigned responsibilities that an individual should handle.

5) Self actualization needs are the needs that place an individual in a stance to fulfill his or her potential, opportunity to seek personal advancement and self realization.

Maslow thus propagated for satisfaction of human needs in the above order to be able to motivate staff properly.

McKinsey came up with the model that would assist managers handle the various issues that could arise during organizational change. The model elaborates the interrelationship between determinants involved during organizational transition. Therefore for any proper change to place in an organization, all these issues must be handled properly.

The model acts as a tool for evaluating organization's strategy and their effectiveness. This model looks into the seven elements that an organization needs to practice in order to emerge successful. The elements in the model have been categorized into two major groups such as hard and soft elements. The hard elements are those that relate to the environment and approach of handling issues while the soft elements relate to the values, skills and style of management, they also include staff of the organization (Mintzberg, & Henry, 2007, p 112).

These elements can be outlined as follows

 ➢ Structure: looks at how the organization is arranged in terms of chains of command, that is who is answerable to whom.

- Shared values: these relate to the values that are common among the members of the company, these values are shown in the corporate culture and the work ethics of an organization.

- Style of leadership: this relates to how the top management leads the organization, that is the management or leadership style that is deemed appropriate by the organization.

- Staff: the employees of the organization also form another very important part of the 7S model, they are human resource that are needed to turn the raw materials into finished goods with the help of machines.

- Systems: these refer to the day to day operations linked together with the duties of the staff within the organization

- Strategy: this refers to the game plan of how to get goals and objectives achieved for the success of the organization.

- Skills: these are the real capabilities of the employees that they apply in handling their tasks and duties in the organization.

The interaction of these elements within the organization determines how an orgnizatio handles it activities and achieves its goals. From this model an organization should incorporate the seven models towards the achievement of organization for each and every business entity, growth is a key component if continuity of the same is to be maintained as well as ensuring minimal losses. If this is to be the case, relevant avenues must be pursued in a logical manner keeping in mind the emerging trends so as to remain top of your league as a business. The management is therefore left no choice but to strategize its operations that ensure the growth beats the challenges encountered (*Pl*Collis, 2004, p 112).

This calls for use of strategic management tools.

The strategies employed by a given a given business address issues specific to the entity and should not be used on a copy paste basis by any other organization. Different management strategies exist and can be employed singly or use in a combination with others to tackle a given challenge or place the user a notch higher than his/her competitors. The chosen tool or tools should serve to ensure better competitiveness, discourage fresh entries into the market and cement a reasonable consumer base for maximum gains (Drucker, 2009, p 109).

Some strategic management tools include but are not limited to;

Strategic planning

This is simply an environment sound approach to planning so as to take into account all relevant dos and don'ts so as to avoid falling victim to barrier imposed by fellow competitors within your line of work. A proper strategy aids to conquer competition thus retain a better market share.

Mission and vision statement

These two serve to bring out the expected results and achievements from the operations of a business. Consumers identify with these statements and are therefore critical in solidifying a wide consumer base which translates to growth of the business or organization thereof (Goold, 2004, p 203).

Customer relationship management

The established customer base requires proper nurturing if it is to remain or better still grow with time. This may call for advertisements and other related services that serve to assure consumers of quality at all times.

Outsourcing

Any business cannot operate in isolation since the market is ever dynamic calling for fresh ideas to be put in place so as to catch up with emerging trends within the field of operation and related business environment. It may be necessary to bring in new technology and manpower so as to create an ideal platform for work (Gottfredson, 2008, p 109).

Core competencies

This refers to areas of best ability for the organization to beat its competitors. It is vital that such abilities and resources required for their execution are maintained and bettered whenever possible to keep a step forward in the market hence acquiring a better command and control of the same.

Customer segmentation

As a business remains in operation, it is able to identify its market and can easily tell its distribution throughout a geographical area. It is profitable to create an atmosphere that tends to offer your customers a feeling of being of a great importance therefore making them want to be associated with the business. This increases their confidence in you and a closer attachment to the business hence cannot be easily swayed away by your competitors (Hamel, 2009, p 119).

With all that in mind, it is necessary to consider the internal and external factors affecting the business before coming up with any strategies. This involves considering the strengths and weaknesses occurring within the organization while at the same time remaining conscious to the opportunities and threats outside the organizations walls (*PlCollis*, 2008, p 78).

Literature Review

The word strategy especially in the business world is a concept that is synonymous to the plan laid down to achieve a defined goal. This concept does not stand the ground to claim its originality from the business field. Researchers and authors have claimed that strategy was borrowed from the arena of military. The Greek used the word in their military setting to refer to the way their military deployed their troops. Strategy in the business field is used to show the direction of organization's policies and activities towards the achievement of a defined goal. The decisions made by the management determine the direction of these policies and activities (Ramanathon, 2003, p 34).

Strategic management however can claim its originality from the business and corporate arena that is strategy and management put together. Strategic management is the process of planning, organizing, and directing a strategy or game that is designed to achieve the organizational goals and objectives. strategic management involves the conducting the following important management activities, conducting an audit of the internal environment, measuring and evaluating performance, implementing strategies, generating and evaluating strategies, establishing the long term objectives, develop the mission and vision statements and finally conducting an audit of the external environment (Stone, & William, 2005, p 103).

Strategic management is dynamic mainly because of the particular aspects such as evaluation and implement that keep on changing from time to time since they are done on a regular basis. The corporate strategy in every organization revolves around its goals and objectives, the achievement of these goals relies on the way a business handles it business strategy and management aspect in its operations (Brown, 2009, p 108).

Authors in the field of strategic management tend to give it a similar approach in definition, however very few of them have come to analyze the benefits of performing particular elements such as evaluation, implementation and external audit in the firm. External audit for instance is performed to identify the opportunities upon which a firm can benefit from and the threats that should be avoided; external audit involves the evaluation of the external environmental factors such as the environmental factors, economic factors, political factors and social factors. Internal audit involves an assessment of the internal activities for instance an assessment of the internal management system or the issues of the organizational infrastructure (Capon, 2010, p 78).

The aspect of competitive advantage as highlighted in this paper involves how a business performs in relation to the environmental forces. These forces are also known as the Porter five model forces, which mainly involves the interaction of the geographical, industry and innovation, the interplay of these factor determine the performance of a business organization in the environment (Cope & Robert, 2005, p 134).

Other strategies of achieving competitive advantage that are not highlighted in background of this paper are retrenchment, divestiture, concentric and horizontal diversification and lastly diversification. It should be noted that while some authors consider retirement as a strategy to achieve competitive advantage, it rips of the organization the best employees who poses the quality skills and competencies, who may secure jobs with the firm competitors and thus become the source of competition in the market. Diversification strategy is applicable where the firm wants to venture into new markets and with new products. Diversification normally takes two forms namely; concentric diversification and horizontal diversification. In concentric diversification, the organization adds new but unrelated products, whereas in horizontal diversification the organization adds new and related products (Friedel, &, Coker, 2009, p 204).

Research methodology: Analysis into business strategy and management control measures for improved competitive advantage.

Introduction

This part played the role of emphasizing possible procedures in addition to the methods that the researcher used to attain the goals of the research objectives and hypothesis for this research. In addition, it also outlined an elaborative site of the work, guidelines for the research and the assessment arrangement that must be addressed in the course of the study when partaking the very research. The research was to commence with comprehension of the research goals besides the analysis. The achievement of the research objectives will rely on adequate data that is in tandem goals and suppositions in the determination of the business strategy and management control measures for improved competitive advantage. The objective of the research just as a review is to identify the business strategy and management control measures for improved competitive advantage. This section elaborates on the types of data collection methods that were used to collect data for this research. It highlights the merits and the demerit that accompanied each method and the way the data for this research was extracted from the respondents. The methods of data collection adopted for this research were relevant the, information received from the respondents were used to answer the research topic Analysis into business strategy and management control measures for improved competitive advantage.

Primary research

This refers to compilation of statistics that is non existent. This was realized through various forms: including the use of questionnaires and by making calls through cellular phones. In this research, the following primary sources were likely to be the existing information about the business strategy and management control measures for improved competitive advantage. The main reason as to why primary research was used for reasons of accuracy and concise. However, the demerit related to the method relates to the fact that, it is in most wastes a lot of time since it the researcher works with a myriad type of respondents. The respondent's data was subject to the willingness of the people interviewed, and this usually took a lot of time to get the information from the respondents' business strategy and management control measures for improved competitive advantage.

Primary method of data collection is the only reliable source of raw data in any research, despite this method being expensive because of the cost elements of transportation, typing and printing the questionnaires it gives the raw actual data from the respondents that can be heavily relied on for the purpose of the research.

The information from this source cannot be doubted because most of the times, the researcher is able to interact with the respondents in person, for instance a scenario where the researcher had the opportunity to interview the respondent bout a particular issue, then in such a case the researcher can question the validity of the information very easily than when the researcher conducted such than relying on the information from already conducted research. Primary research is therefore the most important source of information for any good research that can be relied upon.

Secondary research

In contrast to primary research, this refers to the compilation and utilization information that is already at hand. In this case, it involved the use of researches on experiments or specific subjects which had been studied by other researchers. In this research the secondary source of data include the following, trade journals on business strategy, management books, and information from the internet. Secondary data had the advantage of saving time during data collection. However, information obtained through secondary sources was not very accurate as to meet the objectives of a particular research study. With regards to the current research study, the below listed were secondary data sources. As the name suggests secondary method of data collection does not provide raw data because here the researcher relies on information that had already been searched by other researchers. The validity of data from the secondary sources cannot be easily proved as for the case of primary method of data collection.

i.   Previous researches papers on the subjects of business strategy and management control measures for improved competitive advantage.

ii. Relevant journals and books especially those touching on business strategy and management control measures for improved competitive advantage Relevant internet sources covering information about business strategy and management control measures for improved competitive advantage.

iii.   Other related materials on business strategy and management control measures for improved competitive advantage

The secondary research will provide information that will be used mainly the literature section of this research work. The aforementioned sources were applied and were provided the relevant data needed for the study.

Qualitative and quantitative data

Quantitative data was applied to this research work to be to provide empirical evidence based on the research. Empirical evidence was useful in drawing the conceptual framework of the variables involved in the research. When implementing the activities of any research; qualitative research and quantitative research are applied for they are the most important methods. Qualitative research refers to use of data which is based on meanings obtained through spoken words or personal expressions of the respondents. Use of qualitative data is one of the most important means of answering research questions. In most cases, this technique involves administration of interviews and other oral means of data collection. Qualitative research is one in which the researcher claims some prior knowledge of the research question based on constructivist perspective. This approach uses various strategies of investigation to understand the desired characteristics of the problem such as ethnography, phenomenology, case studies, narratives and studies of grounded theories. Primarily, a qualitative research approach involves the researcher gathering open ended data about the desired phenomenon with the sole intention of developing themes from the data.

Qualitative research approach is a multi-method of focus and involves naturalistic, interpretive approach to answering specific research questions. This, however, implies that a qualitative researcher studies things or phenomenon in their natural settings or perspectives. The researcher will in most cases attempt to interpret his phenomenon characteristics in terms of what they mean to the environment

Qualitative research approach on the other hand is a process that is based on the amount of data collected from study materials. It involves using data that can be numerically described and is appropriate in conducting descriptive researches. In the current research study, this approach will be employed extensively to understand how to apply strategic management for competitive advantage. Application of quantitative approach in research studies produces accurate and up to date information which is not prone to manipulations.

Quantitative research can be defined as research as one in which the researcher uses positivist claims for the purpose of developing specific knowledge. This entails thinking from the perspective of cause and effects and narrowing this down to specific variables, hypothesis and questions .Quantitative research also involves utilization of observations and instruments and analysis of relevant theories on the study subject. The approach utilizes numerous strategies in investigating the research problem such as experimentation and survey and compiles all relevant data on program tools which generate statistically significant data. Due to its nature of approach, quantitative research is often regarded as the hypothesis-testing research. All research hypotheses are derived from theoretical statements and an experimental design is created on which dependent variables are evaluated while controlling for the effects of chosen independent variables.

The corresponding approach that will be incorporated in the current study which will entail random selection of the study population so as to minimize the level of bias and error in analysis of data. An ideal sample of the study population will be drawn and this will reflect the study population. The research steps to be adopted are deductive in nature and this will contribute to understanding of the research problem by testing of the hypothesis. This will be the core characteristic of quantitative research methodology and will entail using factual experimental designs under firmly controlled conditions.

Research Strategy

Research approach will be a wide plan of how the researcher will answer the research questions. It involves clear objectives, resulting from the research questions and denotes the sources from which researcher proposes to gather data and considers the limitations that the researcher will inexorably experience such as limited access to data, time constrains , as well as finances and ethical issues. The strategy enabled the research to lay down a procedure of how to handle the challenges that might arise in answering research the questions. The research strategy gave the research a good approach in handling the research challenges and how to approach them.

Table 1: Research strategies

Strategy	Form of research	Requires control over behavioral event?	Focuses on Contemporary

	question		events?
Experiment	How, Why	Yes	Yes
Survey	Who, What, Where, How many, How much	No	Yes
Archival analyses	Who, What, Where, How many, How much	No	Yes/No
History	Why, How	No	No
Case Study	Why, How	No	Yes

The most vital pre-requisite for the choice of the research approach is the recognition of the type of research question asked. "How", "What", "Why", "Who" and, "Where", these are the cardinal classification methods for the types of research questions. Whichever of these five research approaches can be used in; exploratory case study, exploratory experiment, or an exploratory survey.

Philosophy of the research

Research philosophy is another element that is very vital in the choice of research. It is this aspect that accentuates the whole subjectivity of the research problem in addition to the various research approaches that are utilized in answering corresponding research questions. The selection of the right   research approach shows which methods the researcher approves to answer his objectives or questions. In this particular research study, a positivism philosophy will be used to define and describe the nature of the current research. Essentially, this approach will be used to shed light on how strategic management can enable an organization achieve competitive advantage. This research philosophy will provide indispensable restraints upon which the research uniqueness will be constructed.

In actual facts, an optimistic research attitude enhances collection and utilization of a large amount of data from numerous sources. This fosters reliability and validity of the research findings thus allowing adequate understanding of the research problem. More over, use of grounded theory represents one of the most suitable approaches in which data is collected by way of observation. The data is then evaluated on numerous theoretical frameworks so as to establish the appropriate research strategy, hence enabling the researcher to make substantial prediction about the phenomenon under study and test the research findings to determine whether they support prior beliefs and assumptions on the study problem. Normally, grounded theory serves to make studied data records well prepared and implicit so as to determine the relationships between variables.

The most important research strategies that have popularity in conducting this research are survey. The use of surveys facilitated for the collection of a large amount of data from a large population. This implies that the researcher conducted surveys and to question specific groups of people to obtain large amount of information relevant to the subject of the survey. This was on respect to business strategy and management control measures for improved competitive advantage

the data was collected from the people either via questionnaire or orally. The purpose of the survey was to establish and analyze views of respondents in order to find the views. However, despite the fact that the views from a large number of respondents were gathered through the survey approach the data obtained did not reflect all the objectives of the research at depth.

Case study was also applied in the determination of accurate data. This was a research approach that was considered for the sake of this study which involved investigation due to its applicability in any particular contemporary phenomenon in the real life situation using multiple sources of evidence such as this case. Further detailed clarification on the nature of the case study as a research was an approach that was deemed appropriate was given; case study represents 'a specific way of collecting, organizing, and analyzing data'. Grounded theory embodies a strategy which posits that the data was collected through observations and compared to various theoretical frameworks with an aim of finding out which of the data is the most applicable. This guides the researcher into making predictions about the studied trend prior to testing. However, the objective of grounded theory is to make studied data records well-industrialized and understood and to verify relationships between the findings and the case study in question.

Use of Questionnaires and Interviews

Questionnaires

The reason as to why the researcher used questionnaires to collect the data was for the reason that, questionnaire placed the researcher at stance suitable to amass data from more than one respondent. From a single location this therefore enabled the researcher to minimize the cost associated with travelling many distances in search of the respondents. Questionnaires play the role of enabling the respondent answer the questions with a lot of ease, without any interference thereby enabling the researcher to answer the questions at his or her discretion. Questionnaires are the most applicable method for collecting quantitative data. Before implementing questionnaires it is very important that a pretest is done before the conducting the actual research. A pre-test is very important to enable the researcher to asses the attitude of the respondents so that the researcher can predetermine the type of approach that is used to get the information from the respondents. Questionnaires are classified according to the type of questions that they ask. In this research, the questions asked in the questionnaires were those that were related to the topic of study Analysis into business strategy and management control measures for improved competitive advantage. The questionnaires were distributed to corporate heads, directors, line managers and senior level managers in business organizations.

Interviews

Interviews will be employed in this research so to be a foil for the use of questionnaires the application of interviews was deemed paramount as it enabled the researcher to easily collect the information instantly from the respondent and be to seek clarification where necessary. To fix and control all material circumstances so as to gather all material data while at the same time remaining flexible and responsive to the effect. Interviews were also applied in this research to complement questionnaires. So as to arrive to the purpose of the investigation, the key focus lied on finding out which techniques should be applied. Interviews were the best method for understanding this research. "A respondent interview is one where the interviewer directs the interview and the interviewer responds to the questions of the researcher". And to add more weight on this observation, the use of standard survey interview is in itself essentially an error and that it therefore cannot serve as the ideal ideological model against which to assess other approaches. He also elaborates by describing interviews as the verbal exchange of information between two or more people for the principal purpose of one person or group gathering information from the other. And that Semi structured interviews enable one to fix and control circumstances in order to collect appropriate data while remaining flexible and responsive. In this research, the researcher interviewed the corporate managers, line managers in the organization, and middle level managers. The interview targeted this group of audience because; they are the people who are mostly involved in the formulation of business strategies, and thus were deemed to be the right people who could give the right information pertaining to the research topic Analysis into business strategy and management control measures for improved competitive advantage.

The element of questions in interviews is also another important issue in research, the researcher applied avoided closed open ended questions so as to be specific to the research objectives. The type of questions in a research should were very clear and straight to the point, this was done to avoid the aspect of ambiguity of the questions so that the respondents could easily understand them and therefore answer them with a lot of ease.

Soundness and dependability of the research

This research is vey factual in nature and all research questions are related to the major qualities of the research observable facts as discussed in the literature review. The steps of data collection and further analysis shall therefore be accurate so as to ensure that highest levels of validity are realized. It is however important to note that there are several aspects of research validity which influence reliability of research findings.

There are issues that had been raised by previous researches on the topic of business strategy and management however the3 previous research findings do not at times elaborate the way the data used was collected, their sources and even prove the authenticity of the data. This research exploited the available and most relevant data sources.

Ethical considerations

The concept of ethics in research studies is a very important issue that has been propounded by various philosophers. For instance, Blumberg's explanations can be attributed to the -facts as discussed by Saunders (2003). Saunders defines ethics as the observation of moral principles, norms, values and behaviors which guide interrelationships between human beings at different levels of interaction. In essence, research ethics are observed as a means of marinating the dignity of the research process and that of the researcher and the research participants. Pertaining to this research, the relevant ethical considerations will be given a serious consideration in the process of data collection, analysis and distribution. All the research respondents will be given information before on the research purpose, relevance, benefits and potential consequences of their participation. The data obtained from the respondents will be handled with the greatest level of dignity and integrity. The data will be utilized wholly for the purpose of the research and none shall be disclosed to unintended parties.

The respondents were issued with different questionnaires based on specific areas of interests. The approval or the disapproval of participation relied entirely on its merits and demerits as established after the conclusion of the research. All the respondents were then given their correspondingly informed consent for the reason of participation in the research. They were informed early enough before the conduction of the research, the purposes, the potential benefits as well as the risks that might be associated with their participation. Ethical norms shall be put into consideration in the process of the procedures of the research. The personal information from the respondent was left at the discretion of the researcher and the respondent and therefore not exposed to the public.

In the circumstance that the participants chose not to answer any part of the question/s, their right to not answer were acknowledged and it was ensured that the privacy of any person was not compromised upon. Two attempts were made and no further again to respect the privacy of any individual. More over, the proposals for a general announcement of the ruling for agreeing to contribute to no other involvement incentive were offered. When the researcher was conducting interviews with the sources, researcher was aware of the selected interview time and did not intend to prolong the interview. Essentially, as an important part of the ethical considerations, all the sources of secondary data were given ultimate acknowledgment for their contribution to this study. The data compiled was straightforwardly branded and the investigation was to the best of the researcher's knowledge and capacity. The researcher had to administer the questionnaire at the respondents will and sought permission prior to administering the questionnaire.

Ethics Form for Research Projects

The form should be completed in as much detail as possible. Please submit this form to the module co-coordinator.

Project title:	business strategy and management control measures for improved competitive advantage
Student's name:	
Email address:	
Supervisor:	
Module title/code:	Accounting , Finance and Management

Project Summary: Please be as explicit as possible about methods to be used, including details about participant tasks, especially if these tasks could invoke ethical issues. Attach copies of all measures, tests, inventories, questionnaires and interview questions you intend to use in the course of your research.

Will ethical approval for this project be required from another source? (Organisations such as hospitals, charities and schools may also have Ethics Committees that will also need to approve your work. The responsibility lies with you to check this.).

Yes ❑   No ❑

If yes, what is this source?

Please remember to obtain approval from the other Ethics Committee <u>first</u> and include a copy of this approval in with this form.

INFORMED CONSENT AND DEBRIEFING

Are you aware that participants must give their informed consent to any investigation procedure?
Yes ❑   No ❑

Attach a copy of your participant information sheet, consent form and debriefing and confirm, below, that these provide participants with the following information.

Does this describe the main procedures so that participants know in advance what to expect, including the length of time that their participation will take?	Yes ❑ No ❑
Does this tell participants that their participation is voluntary?	Yes ❑ No ❑
Will you obtain written consent for participation?	Yes ❑ No ❑
Will you tell participants that they may withdraw from the research at any time and	Yes ❑ No ❑

for any reason?	
Will you tell participants that they have the option of omitting any question that they do not wish to answer?	Yes ❑ No ❑
Will you tell participants that their data will be treated with full confidentiality and that, if published, it will not be identifiable as theirs?	Yes ❑ No ❑
Will you make it clear to participants of the categories of people who will have access to their data (e.g. your supervisor) and those who will be reading the final report in an official capacity (e.g., supervisors, examiners, etc.)?	Yes ❑ No ❑
Will you debrief participants at the end of their participation (i.e. give them a brief explanation of the study?	Yes ❑ No ❑

DECEPTION/WITHOLDING INFORMATION
Does your study involve deception or with-holding information? Yes ❑   No ❑
If YES, give a brief explanation and identify how you have confirmed that this is a necessary element of the research.
PROTECTION OF PARTICIPANTS AND RESEARCHER
Are you aware that your study should not expose participants to risks greater than those encountered in ordinary life? Yes ❑   No ❑

Is there any realistic risk of any participants experiencing either physical or psychological distress or discomfort? Yes ❑   No ❑

If YES, then give details and state how you will deal with any problems that arise. Please ensure that this has been thought through carefully and that you are fully prepared for any realistically foreseeable eventuality.

If your study involves answers to personal questions how will you assure participants that they are not obligated to respond?

Verbally ❑ *(this is not sufficient in itself)*

Information on participant Information sheet ❑

In cover information on questionnaire front page ❑

Reiterated on informed consent sheet ❑

Other (please specify)

Are researchers exposed to conditions which may be distressing or present any conceivable personal risk? Yes ❑ No ❑

If YES, what steps have been taken to minimise these? Please note:

If you will be meeting with participants in an informal setting, such as their home or workplace, please discuss issues of your own safety carefully with colleagues or your supervisor. Good practice is to organise officially to inform a responsible person of your whereabouts and anticipated time of return and to contact that person on your safe return from meeting with each participant.

Confirmation of Ethical Safeguards

Project Title
business strategy and management control measures for improved competitive advantage

Student	

Supervisor	

As the **student** who is conducting this research, I have read the Code of Research Conduct and Ethics and completed this form and affirm that appropriate ethical safeguards are in place:

Signature _____ Date _____(Student)

Block capitals _____ (Student)

As the **project supervisor**, I have read the form and affirm that appropriate ethical safeguards are in place:

Signature _____ Date _____(Project supervisor)

Block capitals _____(Project supervisor)

Timeline: Ghant chart

Activity	Weeks																
Week commencing	1	2	3	4	5	6	7	8	9	10	11	12	13	14			
investigate literature	▓																
Writing literature review		▓															
Reading on methodology			▓														
Writing methodology				▓													
Questionnaire design					▓	▓											
Collection of qualitative data							▓	▓									
Collection of quantitative									▓								

Task																		
data										▓								
Analysis of qualitative data											▓	▓						
Analysis of quantitative data													▓					
Writing conclusion														▓				
Submission of first draft															▓			
Revision and submission of final draft																▓	▓	▓

Why use triangulation in research?

Triangulation in research enables the research to identify the difficulties that arise during the data collection methods; it enables the researcher to effectively handle the problem of conflicting results that may arise due to the application of more than one method of data collection. This therefore enables the researcher to smoothly interpret the data to derive the intended result question or object.

Confines in the research

Limitations are a common place phenomenon in every research and these limitations stand the chance of tainting the results of the research. Certain limitations are also attributed to the nature of this research. One of the greatest limitations attributed this research was inadequate research material that made it hectic to access relevant information the topic of business strategy and management. The respondents did not give the questionnaires the seriousness that was expected from them thus leaving certain sections blank. The respondents did not have adequate time to fill the questions and understand the research questions. Finally, certain chunks or sources of secondary research could also be treated as a limitation of the research. This was because of the fact that these sources were not valid or they were not updated therefore the data that was attained from these sources could possibly affect the entire results of the research. Therefore, the researcher took utmost care about all these constraints and tried to minimize them. During the carrying out of the research several challenges were encountered which included:

- Some respondents were not willing to cooperate in the process of carrying out of the interview.
- Some questionnaires were not properly answered while others remained blank forcing the possibility of assumptions to be included here.
- There also existed the tedious and long procedures to be followed in order to obtain the entrance to the premises, some of which were inaccessible,
- A section of the respondents were not willing to fill the questionnaires.

Data collection methods

Data was collected through observation and reports. Direct observation of work presentation was the best method of data collection suitable for this type of research; the respondent answered the questionnaires by filling spaces that they viewed appropriate, with any data collection method that helps in filling of gaps and answer questions. In using this method also it was necessary to ensure that the observations were well arranged in advance and always get permission from top management. Moreover, the workers in these organizations knew the reasons for observing them and in cases where videotaping was permitted, it worked well with the method of data collection.

Through the information gathering process, interviews were contacted in business organizations. This involved interviews on the ability to receive and share data. It also involved interviews to staff officials in these business organizations on how they view the roles of business strategy in achieving the goals of the organization. Adequate question preparation time was used in interviews, to ensure that clear and brief communication is used in each interview, this also facilitated that time and dates were documented precisely. The interviews were documented with as many notes as possible to ensure that all the information was captured. Interviews were used throughout the data collection process, but they were most useful at some point in the performance study point, when one is trying to establish the actual pricing strategies insufficiency. Though time consuming, this process was useful because specific questions were asked and one could ask follow-up questions to get more details on a particular area of interest. For a successful interviewing process in this project, relevant people were contacted and ensure that on questions pertaining business strategy and management were asked i.e. there was need to stick to the main area of study to ensure relevant data is collected throughout the process.

Review of performance data is another method that could be used to gather data. When using this method of analysis, it is important to make sure that the data collected is current because outdated data is as harmful as no data at all. Compliance to restrictions put by the client is also very significant because illegal use of confidential data is illegitimate and detrimental to the users. Documentation on its hardware, security, OS, and networking components is necessary since such information will help in major components of the new information system.

Panel method was also used to collect data, by which data is gathered from the same sample respondent at intervals by either mail or through personal interview. This is normally applicable for longitudinal studies. The period over which panel representatives were contacted for information varied from months to several years and the time interval at which they were contacted over and over again may be 10 to 15 days, or one or two months depending on the type of study and memory length of respondents. This method was successful on collection of data on the same item from the same source over a period of time. The numbers of items were as few as possible in order to be delivered within a few minutes, especially where mail survey was employed. This method required careful selection of well and skilled field workers and effective supervision over their work. This method proved inadequate as a means of data collection for this project because it was very much involving and time consuming. It also required training of field personnel—which was costly and time consuming.

Projective technique is another method of data collection that can be used in this project. It is applicable in cases where direct methods of data collection such as personal, telephone, and mail interviews that rely on respondent's behavior, mind-set etc fails. In cases where respondents are reluctant to converse contentious issues, reluctant to express their true views because of fear of victimization, this indirect method comes in hand as the best solution. It involves motivating respondents for interpretation and in doing so the respondents reveal their inner characters. The basic postulation of this method is that a person gives his own views, ideas and responds to indistinct questions or unstructured incentive resources. Thus, the respondent's insensible operations of the mind are brought to a cognizance level in a hidden and projected manner; therefore, the person is able to project his inner character.

Recommendation

This research is not intended to be used by any government agency in furtherance of any of its objectives but will provide a critical understanding of the subject matter to interested research groups, readers as well as the general public including the government. Appropriate recommendations will be drawn and these will be aimed at;

- lobby groups
- Business entrepreneurs
- Media houses
- Corporate business settings.

Distribution of the Research Results

A research must have the results of what is being investigated and for this research the clearly steps and ways of communicating the results were adopted so that the information could reach the right target audience. This study will look at the management strategies employed by business organizations and the competitive corporate business environment. The research will also be used other researcher in this field.

The results will be communicated through the right channels that will be accessible and reliable to the target audience. Since the audiences targeted by the results are the owners, employees, shareholders and stake holders of corporate organizations, the results therefore can be published in trade journals or trade websites over the internet. The fore mentioned channels were therefore deemed appropriate for the dispersal of research information since the targeted audience could get the information very easily from these channels.

References

Allison, & Kaye.2005. "Why Plan?" *Strategic Planning for Nonprofit Organizations*, New
    York: John Wiley & Sons, . Strategic Planning

Brown, 2009. *How to Shape An Environmentally Sustainable Globe.* New York: W.W. Norton,

Canales, J & Barbara, 2000."One Step Beyond Strategic Planning." *Foundation News &
Commentary*, Vol.41 Issue 5 Sep/Oct. 2000.

Capon, 2010. *Corporate Strategic Planning.* New York: Columbia University Press

Carrigan, &Linda, 2005. "Braking for Growth."Organizational Development.

Collett, & Stacey, 2006. "SWOT Analysis." *Computerworld.*

Cope, & Robert 2005.*Opportunity from strength: Strategic planning clarified with case*
    Washington, D.C.: ERIC Clearinghouse on Higher Education.

Dolence, Michael G., et al., 2005.*Working toward strategic change: A step-by-step guide to
    the planning process.* San Francisco: Jossey-Bass.

Drucker, Peter F 2009.. *Managing in a Time of Great Change.* Harvard Business Press,

Fahey, 2008. *Macroenvironmental Analysis for Strategic Management.*   St. Paul: West,

Friedel, J.N., Coker, D.R., and Blong, J.T. "A Survey of Environmental Scanning in U.S. Technical and Community Colleges." Paper presented at the meeting of the Association for Institutional Research, San Francisco.

Goold, & Michael, 2008. *Corporate-Level Strategy: Creating Value in the Multibusiness Company*. John Wiley & Sons,

Gottfredson, 2006. *Breakthrough Imperative: How the Best Managers Get Outstanding Results*. Collins Business,

Hamel, & Gary, 2009. *Competing for the Future*. Harvard Business School Pres.

Mintzberg, Henry, 2007. *The Rise and fall of Strategic Planning: Reconceiving Roles for Planning*

*Pl*Collis, Daniel J., and Michael G. Rukstad, 2008. "Can You Say What Your Strategy Is?" *Harvard Business Review*, April 2008, *ans, Planners*. Free Press.

Polyack, &Jolene. 2004"Nonprofit Organizations Need Marketing Strategies To Meet Goals." *Business Journal* — Serving Fresno & the Central San Joaquin Valley,

Ramanathon, 2003. *Readings in Management Control in Nonprofit Organizations,* New York: John Wiley and Son's Inc.,

Stone, & William,2005. "Research on Strategic Management in Non-Profit Organizations." *Administration and Society.*